W9-BJC-266

# NEAR-DEATH EXPERIENCES

ENDURING MYSTERIES

KEN KARST

Published by
CREATIVE EDUCATION and CREATIVE PAPERBACKS

P.O. Box 227, Mankato, Minnesota 56002
Creative Education and Creative Paperbacks are imprints of The Creative Company
www.thecreativecompany.us

Design by Danny Nanos of Gilbert & Nanos
Production by Joe Kahnke
Art direction by Rita Marshall
Printed in China

Photographs by Alamy (AF archive, Deco, Science Photo Library), Creative Commons Wikimedia (Ortsmuseum Zollikon), Getty Images (Donald Iain Smith/Moment Open), iStockphoto (BERKO85, jacoblund, kevron2001, markara, montiannoowong, sdominick), Shutterstock (agsandrew, Serhii Bobyk, andrea crisante, Indigo Fish, jurgenfr, lassedesignen, Mike Lemma, luxorphoto, Robyn Mackenzie, mangojuicy, Romanova Natali, Sergey Nivens, Nomad_ Soul, Oranzy Photography, ra2studio, RomoloTavani, SpeedKingz, Taechit Tanantornanutra, Duda Vasilii, Vlue, Igor Zh.)



Library of Congress Cataloging-in-Publication Data

Names: Karst, Ken, author.
Title: Near-death experiences / Ken Karst.
Series: Enduring mysteries.
Includes bibliographical references and index.
Summary: An investigative approach to the curious phenomena and mysterious circumstances surrounding near-death experiences, from survivors' personal accounts to psychological studies to hard facts.

Identifiers: LCCN 2017060033
ISBN 978-1-64026-007-8 (hardcover) / ISBN 978-1-62832-558-4 (pbk) / ISBN 978-1-64000-032-2 (eBook)
Subjects: LCSH: Near-death experiences—Juvenile literature.
Classification: LCC BF1045.N4 K36 2018 / DDC 133.901/3—dc23

CCSS: RI.5.1, 2, 3, 6, 8; RH.6–8.4, 5, 6, 7, 8

First Edition HC 9 8 7 6 5 4 3 2 1
First Edition PBK 9 8 7 6 5 4 3 2 1

CREATIVE EDUCATION • CREATIVE PAPERBACKS

# Table of Contents

Andrew was three and a half years old when he had open-heart surgery. About two weeks later, Andrew asked his mother if he could go back to the beautiful place with all the flowers and animals. “I don’t mean the park,” he said. “I mean the sunny place I went to with the lady.… The lady that floats.” In the account described in Dr. Sam Parnia’s book, *What Happens When We Die*, Andrew told his mother he knew she was outside during his surgery. A year later, while watching a children’s television show about open-heart surgery, Andrew recognized some of the machines. His mother told him he would not have seen any machines, because he'd been asleep during his operation. "I could see it when I was looking down," he insisted, "when I floated up with the lady." Sometime later, when his mother showed him an old photo of *her* mother, who had died before, Andrew identified her as the floating lady. "It wasn't scary. It was lovely," Andrew told his mother. "But I wanted to come back to see you." His mother realized that Andrew had had a near-death experience.

# DESCRIBING THE INDESCRIBABLE

Near-death experiences (NDEs) sound pretty great. You may float above the room. You feel peaceful and happy. Loved ones who have died may come to spend time with you. But there's a big problem with an NDE. You might not live to tell about it.

NDEs got their name because the person who has one must necessarily be near death. The person could be having a heart attack. He or she could be heading into a car accident, or drowning, or falling off a steep cliff. The experiencer might even be declared dead before somehow reviving. That's largely why we don't know a lot about NDEs. The only people who can describe them are those who were about to die or those who were dead but came back to life.

Questions about NDEs start with death. If a person's brain has stopped working, it seems she would not be merely "near" death. She would be completely dead. But if she is not dead, how can she hear and see things going on around her body? Is she somehow not dead, after all? Is there something undetectable by sophisticated hospital machinery that allows people to have such vivid and memorable encounters? Journalist Judy Bachrach rejects the term "near-death" altogether. She calls the people who have these vivid encounters after their bodies have shut down "death travelers."

In the fourth century B.C., the Greek **philosopher** Plato described a soldier's NDE in the *Republic*. Dutch painter Hieronymus Bosch put an image on canvas in the early 1500s that seems to portray an NDE. Swiss **geologist** and mountain climber Albert Heim had an NDE when he was almost killed in a mountaineering accident. He collected tales of similar episodes from 30 climbers, soldiers, and others and published them in 1892.

For much of the 20th century, these incidents were treated as fodder for philosophers and religious thinkers. Today, they continue to be seen as proof of an afterlife or of a caring god. But they also serve as examples of

*After having a near-death experience, people often say they floated above their bodies, saw a bright light, or visited a place that seemed like heaven.*

*Some researchers believe that the feeling of moving through a tunnel during an NDE can be caused by extreme fear and a lack of oxygen.*

the mechanical brain giving way to the higher activities of the mind, or consciousness. Consciousness is like a computer program that is always running in the background of our brains. Brain activity produces emotions, **morality**, creativity, and a sense of the past and future. Some regard consciousness as the human soul.

In the 1970s, **psychologists** began to look at NDEs in a more scientific way. They were interested in how people whose brains had stopped working were able to remember events. How could they hear and see things going on around their body? Psychologists were interested in what that might teach us about death and dying. They were also becoming interested in how these experiences could dramatically change a survivor's personality.

Raymond Moody, a **psychiatrist**, coined the term "near-death experience" in his 1975 book, *Life after Life*. Moody interviewed more than 100 people about strange experiences they'd had while on the verge of death. Their stories were remarkably similar. Moody identified 15 common themes. None of his subjects encountered all of them. And no single event occurred for every subject. The most frequently encountered elements included: hearing oneself pronounced dead; a feeling of profound peace and quiet, or hearing unusual noises; seeing a dark tunnel; being out of one's body and the ability to confirm events seen from that perspective; meeting spiritual beings; being pulled toward a very bright light or light-filled being; a review of one's life; sensing the arrival at a border, then returning to one's life; and the absence of a fear of death.

Moody defined NDEs as "profound spiritual events that happen, uninvited, to some individuals at the point of death." The Dictionary of Modern Medicine says a near-death experience is "a **phenomenon** of unclear nature"

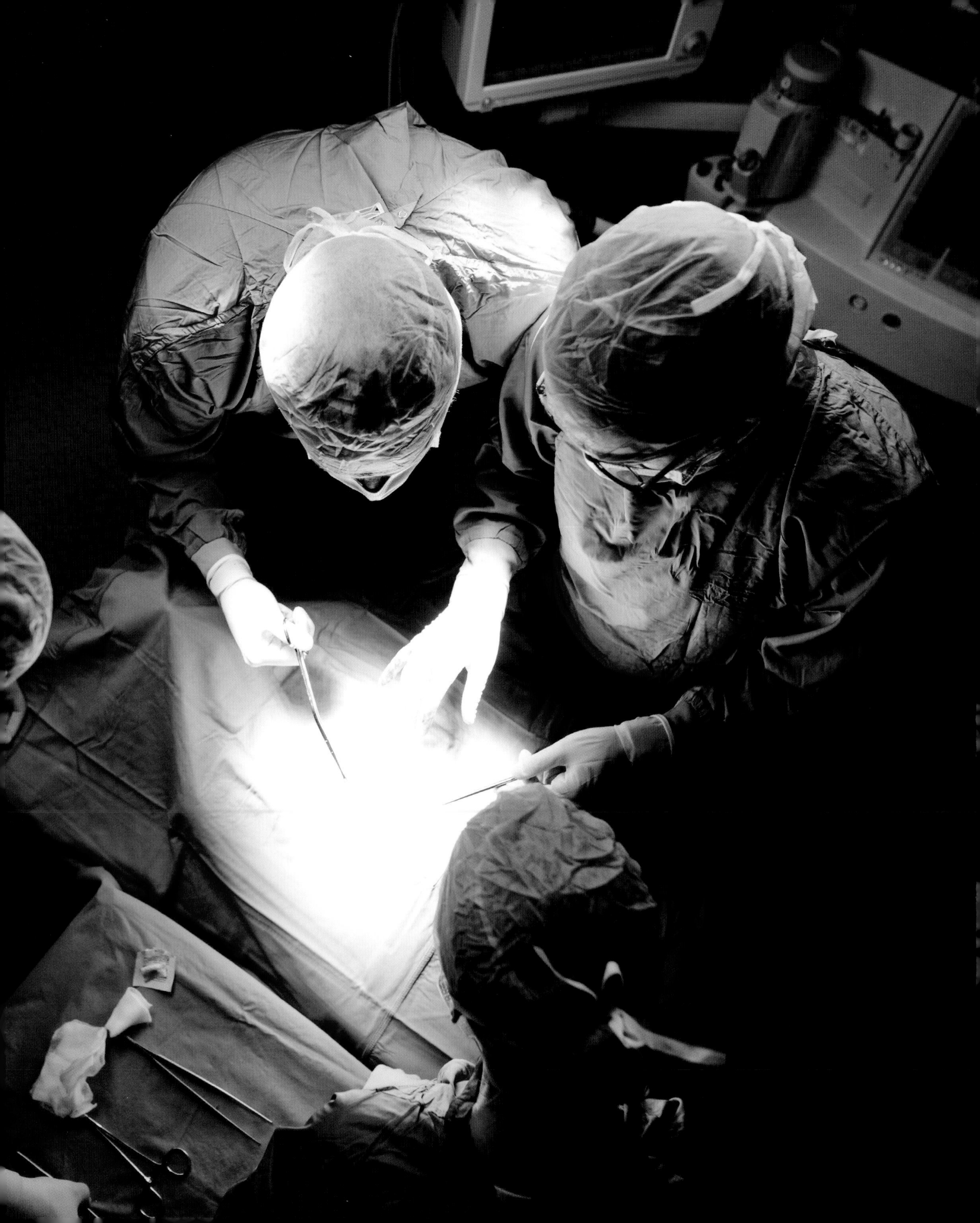

in people without any measurable brain activity. It states that NDEs are "curiosities with no valid explanation." Scientists, though, are in the business of explanation. So they keep trying to figure out what NDEs are, what causes them, and what we might learn from them.

Many scientists are skeptical. Some simply dismiss NDEs as creations of a brain that is struggling with injury, loss of oxygen, or other chemical imbalances. Others shrug them off as an experience of consciousness that can never be measured in any scientific way. NDEs can't be predicted. There is simply no way to know when someone will experience one. This makes them difficult to study. It also means that NDEs can't be understood or tracked in the way that a heartbeat can. As a result, many medical researchers simply don't examine them.

As far as researchers know, not everyone who is near death has an NDE. But many people do. A Gallup poll in 1982 determined that about 4 percent of people in the United States had reported experiencing one. A 2001 poll in Germany arrived at the same figure. But a 2005 poll in Austria reported that 8.9 percent of respondents had had an NDE. A study of heart attack survivors in 2001 found that 6 percent recalled an NDE. Other research has determined that the percentage might actually be higher, between 11 and 23 percent of cardiac arrest survivors.

People from nearly all countries and cultures have reported NDEs. So have people of all ages. NDEs occur to men and women at about the same rate. However, some researchers believe NDEs are slightly different for

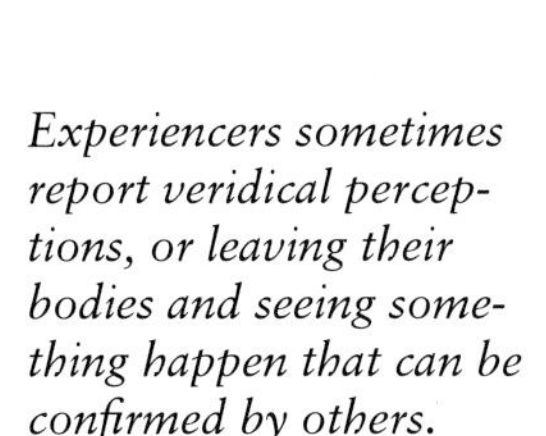

*Experiencers sometimes report veridical perceptions, or leaving their bodies and seeing something happen that can be confirmed by others.*

people from different countries and cultures. This suggests NDEs reflect individuals' belief systems. But the differences are small. Most of the features of an NDE are similar from person to person. "It doesn't matter whether you're a Muslim in Egypt, a Hindu in India, or a Christian in the United States. What you experience will be strikingly similar," says Dr. Jeffrey Long, one of the leading researchers into NDEs.

Experts also point to several things that NDEs are *not*. They are not strictly out-of-body experiences. These can happen to people with **epilepsy** or brain injuries or as a result of exposure to some drugs. While out-of-body experiences are a regular feature of NDEs, they more often occur when people are not near death. Out-of-body experiences can be manufactured, or deliberately caused. But they do not include many of the features of NDEs, such as life reviews or meetings with deceased loved ones. NDEs are also not **hallucinations**, which are often caused by mind-altering drugs or powerful painkillers. NDE experts note that drugs generally cloud people's thought processes, including memory, whereas NDEs make perceptions vivid and memorable. NDEs are not simply dreams, either. We usually forget our dreams. Those we do remember typically do not affect our daily routines. However, NDEs can be life changing.

So are NDEs real? Those who've had one insist NDEs are as real as any other experience. During the NDE, they saw and heard things in the world that others did as well. But they were dead, or close to it. Researchers continue to wonder how, and indeed if, NDEs happen at all.

***The NDE Research Foundation*** The Near-Death Experience Research Foundation (NDERF) maintains one of the most extensive online collections of information about NDEs, including personal stories and research. It was founded in 1998 by Jeffrey Long. He is a medical doctor whose specialty is treating cancers with radiation. Decades ago, Long was looking for articles about cancer when he came across the term "near-death experience." Long became curious. He started collecting stories from people who'd experienced NDEs. Today, the NDERF website contains more than 4,000 accounts of NDEs in 30 languages. It also includes a questionnaire for people to provide the basic outline of their own NDE. Long's wife, Jody, is an attorney and manages the NDERF website. The Longs describe NDEs as profoundly beautiful and comforting. They say death itself is something we shouldn't fear. They strongly believe that NDEs prove that there is a God and an afterlife of all-encompassing love and forgiveness. "Death isn't the end," Jeffrey has said. "I'm convinced, based on evidence, that we're all going to be back together again some day in a very, very beautiful afterlife."

# TRYING TO MAKE SENSE

NDEs make for compelling stories. People who have them may talk about moving through walls, encountering previously unknown relatives, and traveling to places that are beautiful and brimming with love. There they exist in all places and time at once. They are so captivated that they often resist returning to their regular lives.

*Following an NDE, people of all ages have been inspired to capture their visions in art, even if they had not previously been artistically inclined.*

The problem is that these are stories. Researchers have no way to measure these accounts or know what produced the experience. They have no way to determine what NDEs signify about our bodies, our brains, and our minds at death. NDE recollections are similar to one another, but they are rarely identical. Since its development in the 1970s, Moody's checklist has been altered, and even shortened, by numerous researchers. Dr. Bruce Greyson, a former professor of psychiatry at the University of Virginia and a prominent NDE researcher, defines an NDE as a set of "profound psychological events with transcendental and mystical elements, typically occurring to individuals close to death or in situations of intense physical or emotional danger." But author P. M. H. Atwater notes that researchers can't even agree on what they mean by the word "death." Sam Parnia, a British physician and director of the Human Consciousness Project, writes that brain cells can stay alive eight hours after most brain function has stopped. But what the cells generate then, as an NDE or other occurrence, is different from what we regard as thought or perception. So what is death? And what is near death?

Many regard NDEs as religious experiences. Others dismiss them as the products of oxygen-starved brains or overactive imaginations. Less easy to dismiss, though, are the things that happen to people after an NDE. Researchers often focus on these aftereffects, because

they are measurable in some ways.

A common feature of an NDE is the glimpse of some kind of existence beyond our common awareness—life after death. Those who have experienced this say it is beautiful. There is a feeling of enveloping love. They sense that all things are connected and ordered in a way that is beneficial to all. Not surprisingly, people who have an NDE typically conclude that death is nothing to fear. So when they return to their previous lives, they sometimes become risk-takers. One man, an orthopedic surgeon whose NDE was triggered by a lightning strike, bought a motorcycle. He crashed it at a high speed. Then he bought a tractor, drove it into a ditch, and was nearly crushed. "I'm not afraid of death," he said. "I take it to the edge."

That man remained a successful surgeon. But many NDE survivors change their lives entirely. Whether they are accomplished professionals or have never had a career, some find work in fields where they help others. They may go to work in hospice facilities, comforting those who are facing their own deaths. Some survivors develop extraordinary skills. They can predict the future, heal wounds, or recognize that a complete stranger is in an emotional crisis. But it's not all positive. Many NDE survivors find they don't want—or are unable—to describe what they've been through. They feel strange and isolated. Many feel that if they talk about their NDE, longtime friends will think they're nuts.

Researchers have found that NDEs are also hard on marriages. Survivors' spouses may come to think of them as strangers. The spouse often thinks that the NDE survivor doesn't care about the previous years they'd spent together. The survivor loses interest in material things and professional advancement, so many of these couples argue about money. Not surpris-

*Those who return from the brink of death might engage in risky behaviors because they no longer fear dying.*

ingly, researchers report an extremely high divorce rate among NDE survivors—more than 70 percent.

The encounter with some kind of pleasant afterlife or nonjudgmental being can also run contrary to the religious beliefs an individual had before the NDE. Many religious teachings emphasize good works and the punishment of bad behavior. NDEs seem to show that reaching heaven and meeting God, or some heavenly being, is possible for anyone who dies. That newly acquired insight can also drive friends and spouses away from NDE survivors.

If NDEs are as wonderful as survivors say, might people seek them out deliberately? Perhaps. But there is no guarantee that an NDE will be bliss-

ful. Some survivors remember frightening encounters or glimpses of a gray, featureless, meaningless existence. Kenneth Ring is a retired University of Connecticut psychology professor and a leading NDE researcher. He has found that people who have had NDEs during suicide attempts have found them to be briefer and less complex than others. Many people who survive NDEs suffer depression afterwards, regretting that they were pulled back to their familiar lives. However, as Greyson notes, that doesn't drive survivors to suicide. It simply changes what they think is important, making life seem more meaningful. Greyson writes that surviving an NDE usually makes individuals feel closer to other people. This makes survivors feel better about themselves—less guilty and more worthwhile. The NDERF website, a vast collection of NDE accounts and research, makes a point of discouraging people from actively pursuing an NDE. The site says it does not endorse suicide "in any way, shape, or form."

Many children who have NDEs are eager to return to their real lives, often so their parents won't be sad. But because kids have had significantly fewer life experiences than adults, an NDE can have a greater impact on a child. Children often take things personally, so a child might feel rejected or unworthy if he has been "sent back" in an NDE. In her research, Atwater has found high rates of suicide, depression, and alcoholism among adults who had NDEs as children.

NDEs are controversial. They are often dismissed by mainstream scientists. But those who study them have an impressive collection of academic degrees and titles. Many are professors at major universities. There are still plenty of doubters, though. Psychologist Susan Blackmore, a visiting professor at the University of Plymouth in England, argues that NDEs are

*Unpleasant NDEs have involved visions of barren landscapes, feelings of intense heat or cold, and encounters with threatening creatures.*

produced by changes in the brain in the moments before death. They are not evidence of another realm of consciousness. They are not produced by consciousness or by a soul that travels, she writes. Some people say that, based on reports of the sense of moving through a tunnel toward light, NDEs are a recreation of one's birth. Blackmore says this is impossible. A baby can't see as it is being born. And no one can remember birth. Also, people can experience a tunneling sensation during epileptic seizures and migraine headaches, while **meditating**, or while pressing against the eyes. Blackmore and a colleague developed a computer program that, using a simple increase in small specks of light, created a sense of motion for the viewer. The brain might do that when it is dealing with a loss of oxygen. Blackmore also explains that the out-of-body experiences commonly reported by people who've had NDEs are made by a combination of lingering memories and still-active hearing. The life review and blissful feelings common in NDEs, Blackmore adds, could very well be produced by a brain so stressed that it releases an excess of chemicals that produce memories, emotions, and feelings of comfort.

***A Lightning Savant*** Anthony Cicoria is an orthopedic surgeon who was struck by lightning at a family picnic in 1994. He was 42. "I'm dead," he remembers thinking. "Whoever is over there on the ground is a shell." He saw himself turn into a ball of blue light. When Cicoria recovered, he was overcome with an urge to hear piano music, then to play the piano. He started practicing for hours. He would get up at 5:00 A.M. and play before work. After work, he would play past midnight. He also began composing his own music. At the same time, Cicoria began taking unwise physical risks. He was injured in one accident on a motorcycle and another on a tractor. His marriage collapsed. Cicoria continued his professional work. But he also began performing sophisticated classical piano works at festivals and other public events. He even wrote a piece called "Lightning Sonata," which can be found online. He also recorded a CD. Cicoria is what's known as an "acquired savant." That is a person who develops extremely advanced insights or abilities after an injury or disease. A savant is more commonly a person with a developmental disability, such as autism, who has exceptional abilities.

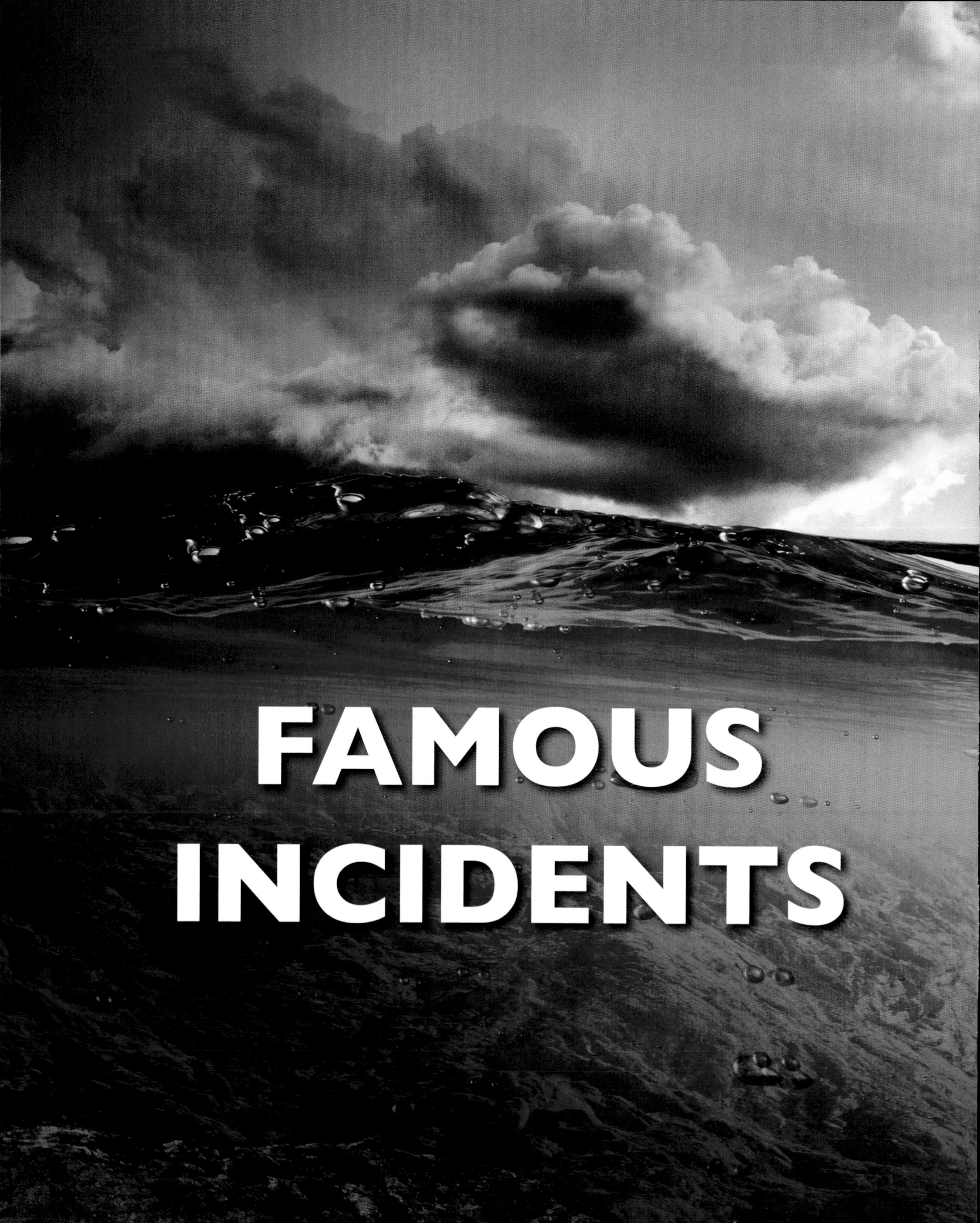

# FAMOUS INCIDENTS

*Plato's* Republic *comprises 10 books (or parts) that discuss justice versus injustice, forms of government, and the eternal nature of the soul.*

In the *Republic*, Plato talks about a soldier named Er. Er died in battle. His body was collected to be burned in a pile with others. But days later, when it came time for the burning, Er sat up, alive. He talked about journeying to a place where the virtuous were rewarded and the unjust were punished. The story was used as proof that the soul never dies. With its journey to a place of light, Er's account is widely regarded as the earliest description of an NDE.

Many such stories have been told throughout history. They often suggest that people's souls go on to another life after they die. As in Plato's story, that's where their performance in this life would be rewarded or punished.

Over time, some of these tales of strange insights in the face of death began to lose the element of final judgment. One involved British Admiral Francis Beaufort, remembered today for his scale for measuring winds. At the beginning of his naval career, when he fell off a boat in Portsmouth Harbor, the teenager did not know how to swim. Years later, Beaufort wrote of struggling in the water and sinking from exhaustion. Then he was overcome with a feeling of calmness, after which every scene of his life appeared to him at once. Both are typical of NDEs.

In 1821, English writer Thomas De Quincey published *Confessions of an English Opium-Eater*. It deals with drug use and addiction, including how opium distorts one's physical senses as well as one's sense of time. It also contains a passage very much resembling what we think of today as an NDE, which De Quincey describes as having been told by a relative of his: "Having in her childhood fallen into a river, ... she saw in a moment her whole life, ... arrayed before her simultaneously as in a mirror; and she had a faculty developed as suddenly for comprehending the whole and every part."

American geographer and geologist Henry Schoolcraft is credited with identifying the source of the Mississippi River. He also studied American Indian cultures in that region. In 1825, he wrote of two Chippewa stories, one involving a warrior killed in battle and the other a village chief who had died. Both stories tell of spirits leaving the men's bodies, wandering, encountering a fiery barrier, and returning to the bodies.

In his 1892 collection of stories of near-fatal accidents, Albert Heim's

findings echoed Beaufort's experience of nearly a century before. "No grief was felt, nor was there paralyzing fright.... There was no anxiety, no trace of despair, nor pain; but rather calm seriousness, profound acceptance, and a dominant mental quickness and sense of surety."

Carl Jung was one of the world's most influential psychiatrists and scholars. He studied spirituality and advocated it as an essential part of each individual. In 1944, following a heart attack, Jung had what many regard as an NDE. In his autobiography, he described seeing Earth from space. He felt as though his entire life's experiences and thoughts existed together. He no longer wanted or desired anything. When his doctor appeared before him, they communicated without speaking; the doctor told Jung he had to return to Earth. Jung was disappointed. He reported other sensations that would make the NDE checklist, including a new and deep appreciation for things as they are. "The visions and experiences were utterly real," he stated.

Pim van Lommel is a former cardiologist and well-known NDE researcher from the Netherlands. He documented a famous case of a man found in a coma in a park. The man was taken by ambulance to a hospital. When he arrived at the hospital, he had no pulse. He was blue. He was not breathing. He had no blood pressure and no brain reflexes. His eyes didn't react to light. Even so, doctors and nurses worked for 90 minutes to **resuscitate** him. A nurse took out his false teeth and put them in a drawer. A week later, the man emerged from his coma (a miracle in itself, van Lommel said). "That nurse knows where my dentures are," the man said, pointing to the nurse. He said she had put them in a sliding drawer in a cart. The cart, he added, had bottles on top of it. The man said he had witnessed all the resuscitation efforts and had been afraid that they might stop. He told doctors

*Jung (above) studied personality, categorizing people according to four basic characteristics: thinking, feeling, sensation, and intuition.*

he had tried to make them aware that he was not dead. His dentures were found right where he said the nurse had put them.

Some scientific studies and accounts of NDEs have led to best-selling books. *Heaven Is for Real* was published in 2010. It's the story of a three-year-old boy's NDE during emergency surgery. The book was cowritten by the boy's father, a Nebraska minister. It tells how the boy, Colton Burpo, encountered a sister his parents had never told him about. (His mother's pregnancy had failed several years before.) He also met a great-grandfather. Colton described some Christian imagery involving Jesus and God as well. By 2014, more than 10 million copies of the book had been sold. It was made into a movie in 2014.

A somewhat similar book, *The Boy Who Came Back from Heaven*, has thrown a cloud over NDE accounts. Alex Malarkey was six years old when he was in a car accident. He was permanently paralyzed and in a coma for two months. He told his parents that he saw angels and met Jesus. His father wrote the book. But in 2015, 11 years later, Alex said the entire account was false; he'd made it up to get attention. The publisher stopped printing the book, which had sold one million copies.

Both books drew criticism from other Christians. One was John MacArthur, an influential **evangelical** pastor and author of 150 books. "All these supposed trips to heaven are hoaxes, and they prey on people in the most vulnerable way, because they treat death in a superficial, deceptive fashion," he told the *Guardian* newsmagazine.

*The film version of* Heaven Is for Real *was nominated for Teen Choice and People's Choice awards.*

Meanwhile, NDEs are a plot fixture in the Netflix series *The OA*. The main character, in fact, is sighted after having been blind, an option she chose for herself in an NDE. (NDE survivors often come back changed but

usually not so dramatically.) In literature, a fictional account of something resembling NDEs reached bestseller lists in 2017. George Saunders's novel, *Lincoln in the Bardo*, spins a tale involving president Abraham Lincoln's dead 11-year-old son Willie. After Willie died of typhoid fever, the grief-stricken Lincoln visited his son's temporary tomb the night after his funeral, holding the boy's body in his arms. That much is fact. But most of the book's narrative is fictional. The main characters are the colorful but confused residents of the cemetery, who don't quite know they're dead. They exist in the bardo, a Buddhist conception of a place between death and rebirth. Unlike NDE survivors, the characters in the book don't return to their previous lives. But they do undergo life reviews and are clearly in the midst of some kind of conscious episodes.

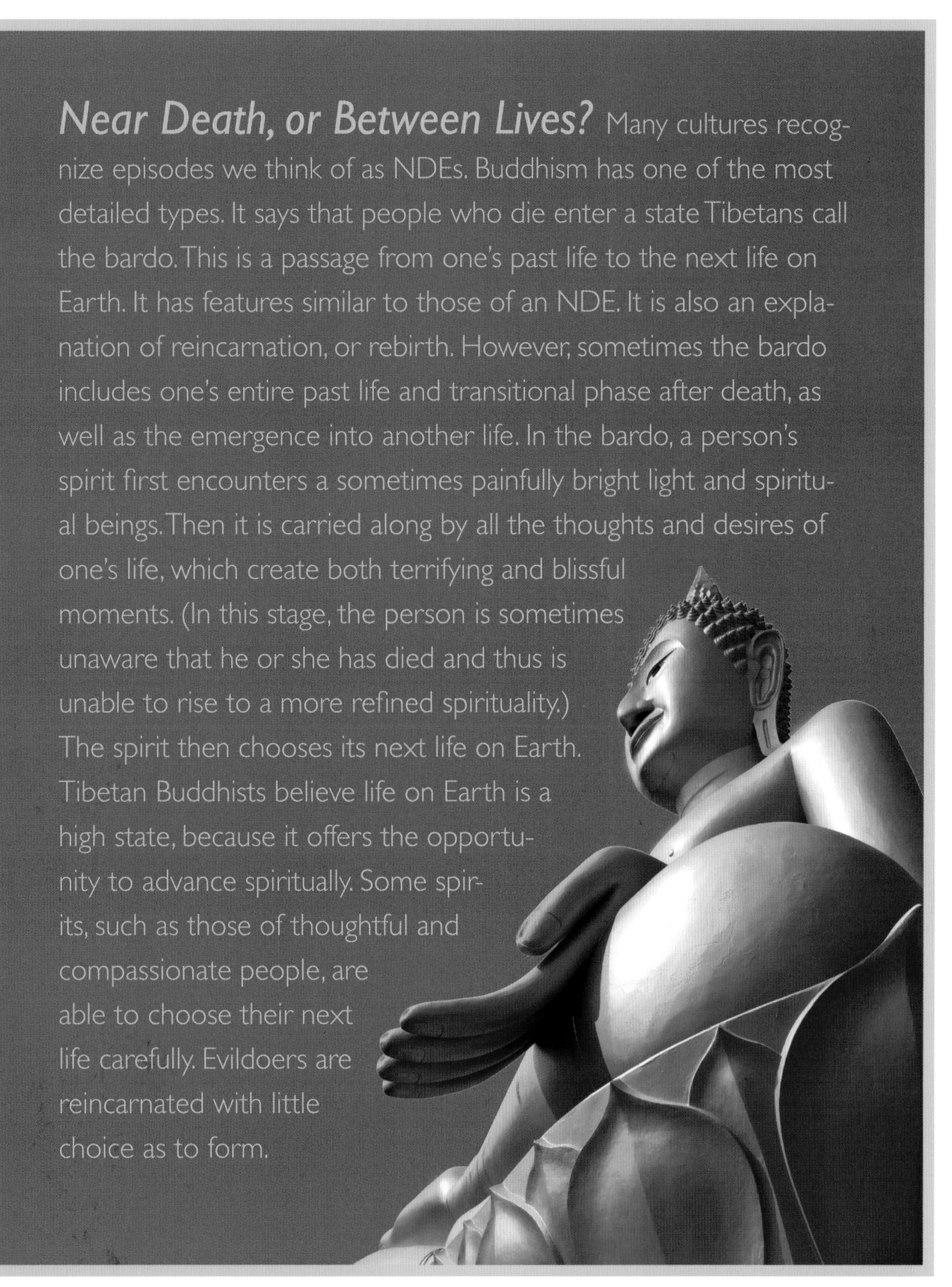

***Near Death, or Between Lives?*** Many cultures recognize episodes we think of as NDEs. Buddhism has one of the most detailed types. It says that people who die enter a state Tibetans call the bardo. This is a passage from one's past life to the next life on Earth. It has features similar to those of an NDE. It is also an explanation of reincarnation, or rebirth. However, sometimes the bardo includes one's entire past life and transitional phase after death, as well as the emergence into another life. In the bardo, a person's spirit first encounters a sometimes painfully bright light and spiritual beings. Then it is carried along by all the thoughts and desires of one's life, which create both terrifying and blissful moments. (In this stage, the person is sometimes unaware that he or she has died and thus is unable to rise to a more refined spirituality.) The spirit then chooses its next life on Earth. Tibetan Buddhists believe life on Earth is a high state, because it offers the opportunity to advance spiritually. Some spirits, such as those of thoughtful and compassionate people, are able to choose their next life carefully. Evildoers are reincarnated with little choice as to form.

# THEY CALL IT "NECRONEU-ROSCIENCE"

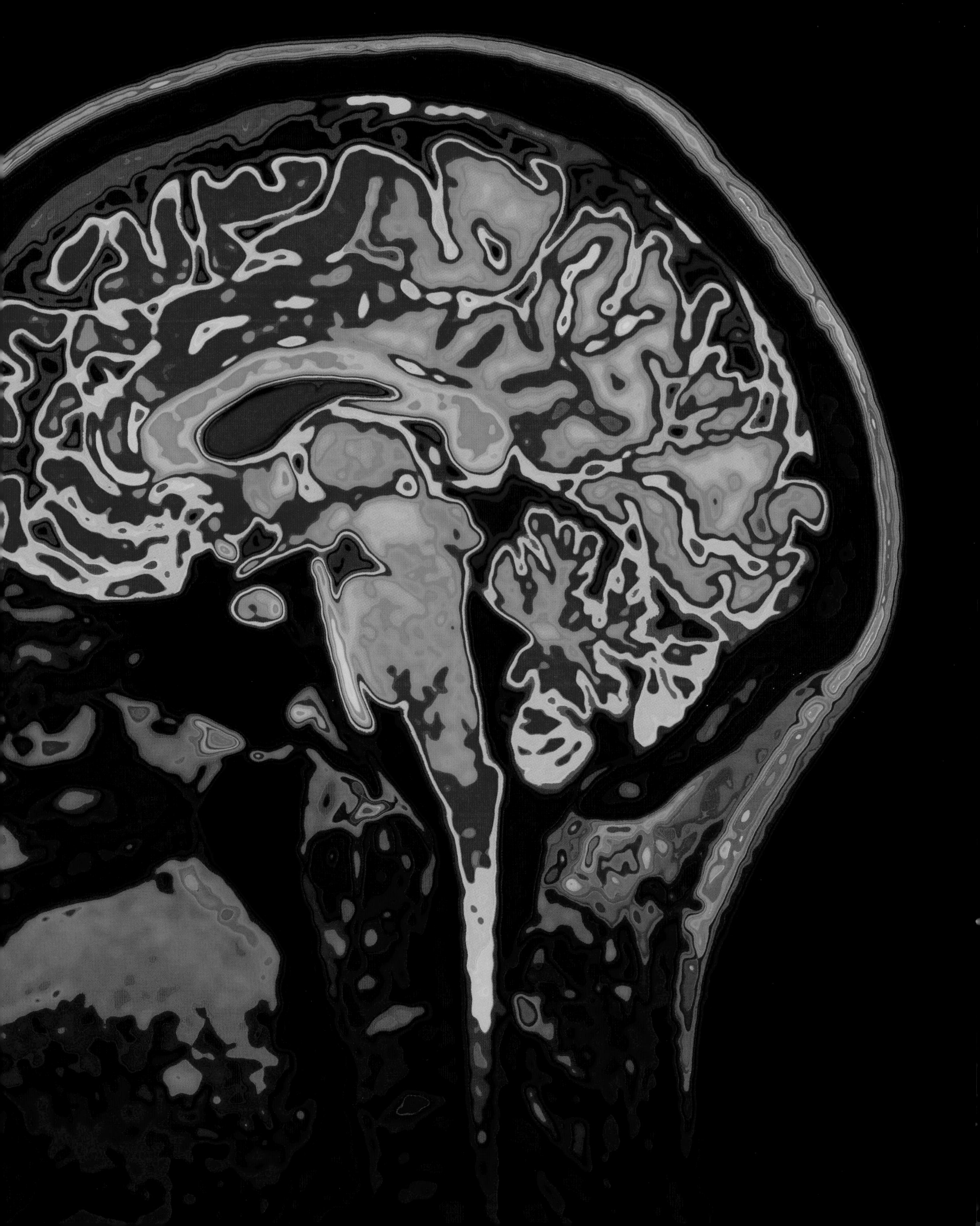

*Researchers' attempts to capture rats' brain activity at the onset of death have garnered mixed reactions from scientists and animal rights activists.*

Nine laboratory rats at the University of Michigan may have led the way to a better understanding of NDEs. In 2013, these rats weren't scurrying around the laboratory looking for food. Instead, they were facing a death sentence in the name of science. Scientists planted electrodes in the rats' brains and then gave them deadly injections. Using the electrodes, the scientists measured the rats' brain activity at the point of death. The scientists were astonished. The rats' brain activity actually increased briefly after their hearts stopped.

The experiment was part of an emerging field of science studying the brain during and after death known as necroneuroscience. The term combines "necro," meaning death, and "neuro," referring to the nerves or nervous system. One scientific journal described it as a field "where no one really knows what's actually going on." That was a lighthearted way of saying it holds the possibility of new discoveries.

The rat researchers thought it might be possible that humans also see a brief increase in brain activity after they die. That might yield a scientific explanation for NDEs. It could show that NDEs are produced by enhanced brain function after the moment of death. Those lucky enough to be resuscitated, or to escape death some other way, might remember NDEs as a series of events in which they had somehow participated. However, NDEs might be the result only of a burst of chemicals in the brain, similar to what the rats showed. "It may mean that the brain goes into a final, hyperactive spasm when its oxygen supply is cut as it tries to figure out what is happening," wrote journalist Gideon Lichfield in a 2015 article in the *Atlantic*. "If so, that heightened activity might

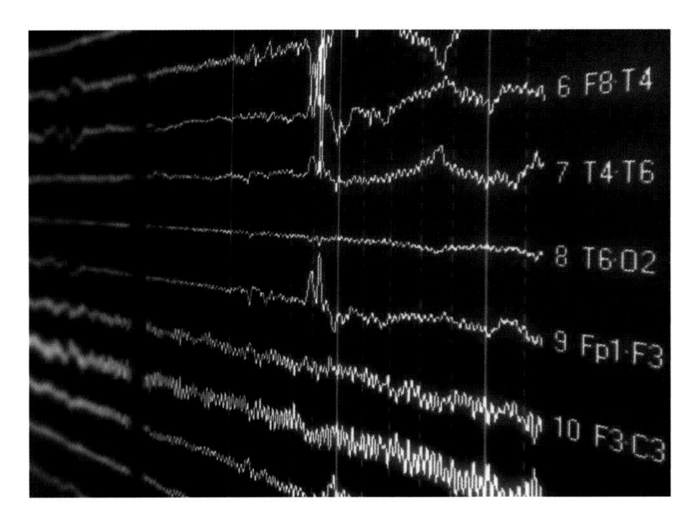


explain why people who say they had an NDE report that what they experienced seemed more real than the physical world."

Jimo Borjigin, one of the rat study researchers, echoed that idea. An NDE, she says, "perhaps is really the byproduct of the brain's attempt to save itself." Even then, concluding that an NDE might be the result of a brain-wave blast doesn't mean an NDE isn't real.

Parnia claimed the rat test was inconclusive. Rats aren't humans, he noted. No one would ever be able to figure out if a rat had an out-of-body experience, met rats who had died before, or had a review of its life. It's also unlikely that any such test might be done on humans. Deliberately letting a human subject die, or even approach death, as part of a test would be considered unethical.

It so happens, though, that human brain activity during death actually has been studied in a small sample. Four terminally ill patients in an intensive care unit at Canada's University of Western Ontario were tracked in the minutes until and after their hearts stopped beating. One of the patients showed brain activity 10 minutes after death at a level similar to that of deep sleep. The four patients showed that brain activity ceases at different rates. This suggests that the experience of dying might be significantly different from one person to the next.

Scientists will never draw broad conclusions from so few subjects, though. In fact, the apparent variations in how brains continue to work after death raise all kinds of other questions. The first, obviously, is how

*Despite multiple efforts to determine the validity of NDEs, we might not ever know the answer to this mystery.*

we define death. Death is commonly regarded as occurring when the heart stops beating. But what if brain activity carries on? Does that mean the person might still be conscious, or in some way still experiencing life? And if so, does that mean doctors should be more cautious about declaring a person dead? Should they wait before harvesting organs? If doctors delay too long, some organs would be wasted and thus not available for transplant to save other patients.

Research into NDEs continues to come up against obstacles. Case studies are done after the event. Many patients are reluctant to discuss their experiences. Details are lost, forgotten, or distorted. One example of the difficulties researchers face is a study Parnia designed at the suggestion of pioneering NDE researcher Peter Fenwick. Parnia arranged to have objects or pictures installed near the ceilings in cardiac units in 15 hospitals in the U.S., the United Kingdom, and Austria. The idea was that patients floating above their bodies at death might see these things. The items would not be visible to anyone on the floor. In fact, the staff was often never informed that the objects were there. But not a single patient saw one. The study had another bit of bad luck. Of the 2,060 patients Parnia studied over 4 years, 330 survived cardiac arrests. Of those, 140 agreed to be interviewed. A preliminary screening left 101 subjects for the study. Of those, nine had NDEs, using Greyson's scale. Only two recalled out-of-body experiences. One became too ill to continue with the study. The remaining patient, a 57-year-old man, recalled details of his resuscitation that would have occurred 3 minutes after his heart stopped. He might have advanced the research dramatically. But the room he'd been in didn't have any of the objects or pictures installed near the ceiling. So there was no way to know exactly what he might have seen when he was allegedly floating above his body.

Without a strong scientific explanation or experiments that can be controlled, NDEs don't get much of the science spotlight. That doesn't seem to bother most experiencers, as many people who believe in NDEs are indifferent to science. So NDEs continue to be widely regarded as expressions of religious or spiritual beliefs.

*The popularity of books and movies about NDEs reflects society's interest in the unexplainable.*

Some put NDEs on a middle ground. Mayo Clinic College of Medicine, for example, offers a class on NDEs to first-year students. In the organization's own words, the course covers the point "where science and spirituality meet." It focuses on how doctors—both those who accept NDEs as a valid experience and those who don't—might deal with reports of NDEs

professionally, with both patients and colleagues.

NDEs may be on the verge of getting more attention in an unexpected way. As we turn more and more of our lives over to computers, that technology raises many of the same questions that NDEs do. They force us to think about consciousness. Does a robot have consciousness? Is that what "smart" means? Does a driverless car, which makes its own decisions, have consciousness? At what point does a calculating machine become more like a mind, or a conscious thing?

What is consciousness, anyway? Even scientists don't agree on one answer. How is it that when we "lose consciousness" we're not aware of anything, but when our hearts stop and we enter an NDE, we can be aware of so much? Why do fighter pilots, who can lose consciousness while turning at high speeds, report feelings of **euphoria** and separation from their bodies but no life review? Is consciousness something that exists apart from the individual? Is it somehow shared with others? Or is it unique to each individual, reflective of one's perceptions and experiences?

"In our lifetime we will figure it out," Parnia says. "We will know what's happening."

***Measurable Aftereffects*** The first surprise for people returning from an NDE is often that they've returned at all. But other surprises soon follow. One unusual aftereffect of an NDE is a change in the **electromagnetic** field around the person. This is unusual because it's measurable, noted researcher Penny Sartori. People often find their watches have stopped after an NDE. Lights will flicker when they're in the room. Toasters, computers, and credit card readers will stop working. Some NDE survivors have miraculous recoveries from advanced illnesses. Others even develop a power to heal. Some become able to "see" events before they happen, often experiencing an event as if it were a memory. Researcher P. M. H. Atwater writes that this may be because NDE survivors develop a new understanding of how time works. Other survivors report that they become aware of the thoughts of the people around them. Abilities like these may provoke laughs from some or wonder from others. But friends, relatives, and strangers may find them frightening. Loved ones may also come to expect special favors from the person with those abilities, such as help with investing money. So NDE survivors are often reluctant to talk about any newfound skills.

# Field Notes

**electromagnetic:** having to do with magnetism created by a current of electricity

**epilepsy:** a neurological disorder most often marked by seizures

**euphoria:** a feeling of intense confidence, happiness, and well-being

**evangelical:** belonging to a tradition within Protestant Christianity that emphasizes belief in the Bible as being the true word of God and a personal conversion to faith

**geologist:** a scientist who studies the physical components of the earth

**hallucinations:** physical perceptions of things that do not exist outside the mind

**meditating:** thinking deeply or concentrating on an idea, sound, or image in order to clear one's mind of distractions

**morality:** good conduct, or a system of rules or values for good conduct

**phenomenon:** an occurrence that can be observed

**philosopher:** a person who examines or develops systems of beliefs

**psychiatrist:** a doctor who diagnoses and treats mental illnesses

**psychologists:** people who study the mind and its functions

**resuscitate:** revive from death or unconsciousness

# Selected Bibliography

Atwater, P. M. H. *The Big Book of Near-Death Experiences: The Ultimate Guide to What Happens When We Die*. Charlottesville, Va.: Hampton Roads, 2007.

Bachrach, Judy. *Glimpsing Heaven: The Stories and Science of Life after Death*. Washington, D.C.: National Geographic, 2014.

Greyson, Bruce. "Biological Aspects of Near-Death Experiences." *Perspectives in Biology and Medicine* 42, no. 1 (Autumn 1998): 14–32.

Lichfield, Gideon. "The Science of Near-Death Experiences." *Atlantic*, April 2015.

Parnia, Sam. *What Happens When We Die: A Groundbreaking Study into the Nature of Life and Death*. Carlsbad, Calif.: Hay House, 2006.

Sartori, Penny. *What Is a Near-Death Experience?* London: Watkins Media, 2016.

# Websites

INTERNATIONAL ASSOCIATION FOR NEAR-DEATH STUDIES, INC.
https://www.iands.org/home.html

NEAR-DEATH EXPERIENCE RESEARCH FOUNDATION
http://www.nderf.org/

*Note: Every effort has been made to ensure that any websites listed above were active at the time of publication. However, because of the nature of the Internet, it is impossible to guarantee that these sites will remain active indefinitely or that their contents will not be altered.*

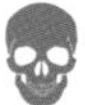

# Index